CAREER SKILLS LIBRARY

INFORMATION MANAGEMENT

CAREER SKILLS LIBRARY

INFORMATION MANAGEMENT

by Joe Mackall

A New England Publishing Associates Book

Copyright ©1998 by Ferguson Publishing Company, Chicago, Illinois

Printed in the United States of America
U-8

Library of Congress Cataloging-in-Publication Data

Mackall, Joseph.
    Information Management / by Joseph Mackall.
       p. cm.
    Includes bibliographical references and index.
    Summary: Explains how to retrieve and evaluate information as well as how to use it effectively in writing reports and making presentations.
    ISBN 0-89434-215-0
    1. Information retrieval—Juvenile literature 2. Research—Methodology—Juvenile literature. 3. Business report writing—Juvenile literature.
    [1. Information retrieval. 2. Research—Methodology 3. Report writing.] I. Title
    ZA3060.M33   1998
    001.4—dc21   97-26635
                                               CIP
                                               AC

CONTENTS

INTRODUCTION

The Information Age is upon us. It seems that the word "Internet" is the second or third word in every sentence spoken or written nowadays. Suddenly 35 million people can sit in their family rooms and e-mail somebody in China or search through the shelves of a university library in England. We all have access to the same information, and there's a lot out there.

It is a very sad thing that nowadays there is so little useless information.
—Oscar Wilde (1854–1900),
British Poet and Playwright

It used to be that having access to information was what separated the educated from the uneducated. Either young people had the money to attend college (where nearly all information used to be), or they didn't. Having access to what we know about the world used to be the key to a young person's success.

Now nearly everybody can have access to the same information if they have access to a computer and a modem. So then we will all be just as prepared for

Today, advanced technology such as accessing the Internet makes an abundance of useful information available to everyone. A century ago, British poet and playwright Oscar Wilde already was commenting on the information glut.

the future, right? Of course not. More than at any other time in history, we have to know what to do with all the information out there. *All information is not created equal.* You need to learn how to acquire information, and then how to evaluate it, organize it, maintain it, and present it. You must be able to see how you have been performing these information management skills your whole life. You also must learn how to do it better.

Scott begins his busy day as a real estate consultant trying to catch up with what has happened since he last sat at his desk.

"I feel like I'm behind even when I get to work early," Scott said. "I'm going to need to set up a cot next to my desk."

By the time Scott has checked for faxes, e-mail messages, voice-mail messages, and old-fashioned letters, documents, and memos that have come in since he left work the day before, his first hour of work is gone, and he still has to act on this new information. He has to answer some of it, file a portion of it, think about a lot of it, and throw a few things away.

A recent study by the Institute for the Future, the Gallup Organization, Pitney-Bowes, and San Jose University in California discovered what Scott and most people in schools and offices already know. The study found that thanks to all the new technology, most of us are experiencing communication gridlock.

The study was based on responses from more than 1,000 employees of Fortune 1,000 companies. It found that workers send and receive an average of 178 messages each day. These messages are sent and received by technology we did not even have until recently: e-mail messages, voice mail, faxes, and pagers.

Workers send and receive an average of 178 messages each day.

The telephone accounted for 24 messages a day, and e-mail and voice mail were responsible for 25. When you think of Scott finally catching up after an hour on the job, think of this. According to the study, Scott and 84% of other workers will be interrupted by new information at least three times every hour.

You already know that information is coming at us at a rate unprecedented in history. Just turn on your TV or log on to the Internet and you will be reminded of just how much information is out there. So being able to manage this information could be the deciding factor between making it and not making it in the next century.

This book is designed to help you handle living in the Information Age. It will show you how skilled you are already at many facets of information management, and it will give you some tips on how to do these things even better. The book deals with such important aspects of information management as acquiring and evaluating information, interviewing, observation, computer research and storage, library research, the Internet, and the World Wide Web.

Perhaps, most important of all, it will give you a general introduction to the basic technological tools businesses use to manage information, such as spreadsheets, databases, and word-processing programs.

The book also will introduce you to people like Scott, rookies in the workforce who are doing well in their chosen careers but who had to learn a few things about information management the hard way. Part of their contribution to this book is to make sure you do not have to learn the same way they did.

CHAPTER ONE
WELCOME TO THE INFORMATION AGE

Millions of years ago, a creature with hair covering 99% of his body woke up, scratched himself—practically everywhere—and looked around. He had no idea that he was living in the Pleistocene epoch.

He didn't know in which time he was living for a couple of reasons. The first reason was because his brain was much less developed than your brain, and a less developed brain can hold less knowledge. The second reason the hairy man (if you can call him that) didn't know he was living in the Pleistocene epoch was because historians and scientists had yet to come along and give the period its name.

But we don't need historians or scientists to tell us we are living in the Information Age. All we need to do is look around. There is hardly a house in the United States that doesn't have at least one TV. Some of these televisions have hundreds of channels. Satellite dishes beam in signals from around the world. Fax machines

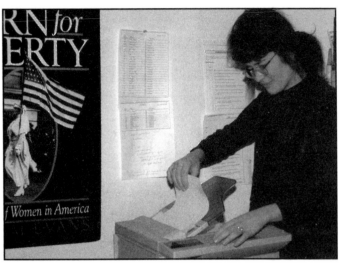

(V. Harlow)

Living during the Information Age means you can and must locate, use, and store information quickly. With the use of a facsimile machine, you can send pages of information to someone next door or to someone halfway across the world in a matter of seconds.

send pages of information from a city in Alaska to a country in Africa in a matter of seconds. More information can be stored on a computer chip the size of a freckle than can be stored in a roomful of file cabinets.

All of the books in the world contain no more information than is broadcast as video in a single large American city in a single year. Not all of the bits have equal value.
                                        —Carl Sagan, Astronomer

*The medium, or process, of our time—
electronic technology—is reshaping and
restructuring patterns of social independence
and every aspect of our personal life.
It is forcing us to reconsider and reevaluate
practically every thought, every action, and
every institution formerly taken for granted.
Everything is changing—you, your family,
your neighbors, your education, your job,
your government...And they are changing
dramatically.*

**—Marshall McLuhan,
Canadian Educator
and Author**

There are more than 60 million pages of information currently on the Internet's World Wide Web.

And if this weren't enough, there's the Internet. The Internet is the name for the vast collection of interconnected computer networks around the world. By typing a word into a slender rectangular box, millions of pages of information are instantly at your disposal. According to a recent article in the *Kansas City Star,* there are more than 60 million pages of information currently on the Internet's World Wide Web—and that number expands by millions of pages every month!

DAILY INFORMATION

Although the vast amount of available information can be daunting, you have been acquiring, evaluating, organizing, maintaining, interpreting, and communicating information all of your life. You've learned something about the past by listening to your parents

---

WHICH OF THESE WILL HELP YOU FIND OUT ABOUT IGUANAS?

1. Talking to the pet store manager about iguanas.
2. Reading about them in your encyclopedia.
3. Looking them up on a CD-ROM.
4. Watching what they eat.
5. Talking to your friend who has one.
6. Doing a word search on "iguana" on the Internet.
7. Dangling an iguana in your grandmother's face on Thanksgiving.
8. Spending an hour watching iguanas at the pet store.
9. Watching a documentary on the mating habits of iguanas.
10. Holding and petting an iguana.

(Joe Duffy)

"Excuse me, waiter, but there's <u>NO</u> fly in my soup."

telling stories about their childhoods. You know your best friend's favorite football team. You've searched through pages of the newspaper to find exactly which movie is playing at what time at the cinema closest to your house. You've learned how a puppy becomes an adult dog by living with it and taking care of it. You know how long it usually takes a wound on your arm to heal.

19

In short, you've used and continue to use the basics of information management almost automatically on a daily basis. When you looked through the newspaper to find the movie, you were searching a document. You discovered your friend's favorite team by using interviewing techniques, and you learned a little something about the healing process by observing the scratch on your arm as it changed from open skin, to scab, to new skin.

Although at least nine of the items on this list are solid sources of information, even the seventh—dangling an iguana in your grandmother's face during Thanksgiving dinner—can tell you something about them. For instance, you can learn how iguanas react when somebody screams. Do they try to scamper away? Do they close their eyes? Do they freeze up? After your grandmother recovers, you can interview her about the experience. She could tell you what about the iguana scared her. Maybe her feelings reflect the feelings of other people, which could help explain why more people in America have dogs and cats as pets than iguanas.

KEY TERMS AND CONCEPTS

This book will introduce you to many information management terms and concepts. In particular, it will discuss:

- acquiring and evaluating information
- organizing and maintaining information; and
- interpreting and communicating information.

Acquiring and Evaluating Information Although Chapters 2 and 3 spend more time on these concepts, let's take a look at one way we acquire and evaluate information on an ordinary weekend.

Take the movie example we talked about earlier. You have a goal. You want to find out if a particular movie is playing. You also want to know what time it's playing and where. Immediately, you have decisions to make. You could ask your brother who went to the movies last week. You could ask your friends or your parents. You could check the Internet. You could pick up the phone and begin calling local theaters. Or you could find the movie section in the newspaper and search the listings.

Say you choose the newspaper. You locate the movie listings and find your movie. You're delighted that the movie you're dying to see, *The Night of the Barney-Hungry Iguana,* is showing at the only theater within walking distance of your house. You're just about to call a friend when you notice the date on the newspaper. It's a week old. It's possible, maybe likely, that the movie information is out of date. You search the house for this morning's paper and find that T*he Night of the Barney-Hungry Iguana* is playing at another local theater.

In this ordinary scenario, you have decided what you needed to know, acquired the information and evaluated it for relevance and accuracy.

This same process is played out in schools and businesses all over the country. The information may be different; the process may be a bit more complicated but the basics are the same.

Organizing and Maintaining Information Putting these in their simplest terms, organizing and maintaining information means keeping track of information in some kind of systematic fashion.

Take Chris, for instance. Chris has just finished his second year as a junior stockbroker. He learned a great deal about business and marketing in his part-time jobs during high school and from his courses in college. But there was one important aspect of his job that he'd been practicing since he kept a baseball card collection in an old shoe box. For most of his years in grade school and even into high school, Chris collected baseball cards. However, his hobby went far

\

EXERCISE

1. Write these sentences down on a sheet of notepaper and fill in the blanks:

   a. I could develop a filing system for my _____ by _____.

   b. A computerized record-keeping system could help me organize my _____ by _____.

Or:

2. Describe an opportunity at your part-time job for improving efficiency by developing a printed or computerized information storage system.

beyond collecting the cards of his favorite players.

"I loved keeping track of how a card's worth went up or down," Chris said. "I got a rush out of trying to guess who would be worth what and when. I had a pretty elaborate system worked out, for a kid that is."

According to Chris he would print a player's name in the left-hand column of a piece of paper. He then wrote 5 or 10 consecutive dates across the top of the rest of the page and drew lines separating them. By keeping these sheets of paper tacked to the back of his bedroom door, Chris needed only to check the price list for a given player in any given year and add the worth of the card to his records. By adding up the totals, Chris could discover at a glance and with a quick calculation what his collection was worth. Even at a young age and without knowing it, Chris was using a spreadsheet. (Spreadsheets are discussed in detail in Chapter 4.)

"I had trouble keeping a straight face at meetings when my bosses talked to me about computer spreadsheets," Chris said. "I just kept thinking of those yellowed pages tacked to my bedroom door."

Successful information managers, however, keep their minds and their options open.

Depending on their personality, education, or experience, some people seem to get locked into one way of acquiring information. Successful information managers, however, keep their minds and their options open.

Interpreting and Communicating Information In his book *The Call of Stories,* psychiatrist and writer Robert Coles recounts his first years as a psychiatrist. He had the devotion and the education. He was ready to take on the world of psychiatry and the people in it. But the more he reported on his patients to his superiors, the more one elderly psychiatrist in particular wanted to hear the stories of Coles's patients. He didn't want Coles to read medical jargon from a chart; he wanted to hear the stories these patients had to tell. And so Coles began listening to—and telling—stories.

Ironically, Coles had grown up in a home where stories were read and told all the time. His parents had read all the "classics" and often told their son versions of these tales as bedtime stories. But by the time he earned his degree and then joined the work-force, Coles seemed to forget how important narrative is to communicating information.

As we'll see later in this book, stories, of course, are not the only means of interpreting and communicating information. It is important to be aware of and schooled in as many ways of presenting information as possible. Depending on your audience, purpose, and goals, you may choose a multimedia presentation, or a simple oral presentation; you may use overheads, slides, graphics, or audio.

The man who succeeds above his fellows is the one who, early in life, clearly discerns the object and towards that object, habitually directs his powers. Even genius itself is but fine observation strengthened by fixity of purpose. Every man who observes vigilantly and resolves steadfastly grows unconsciously into genius.

**—Edward George Bulwer,
English Novelist**

PUTTING IT ALL TOGETHER

As we saw in the example above, there are nearly as many ways to communicate information as there are types of information. One ambitious young woman discovered she needed a variety of ways to present the information about why she was the best person for the job.

Jill was a 21-year-old woman when her father asked her if she'd run his roofing business for a few weeks during the summer while he was recovering from a minor operation. Jill was astute enough to anticipate the suspicious looks she'd get from potential customers used to seeing a man climbing out of a roofing truck.

Jill had acquired a lot of information about the roofing business. She'd kept her father's books for a couple of years and had even interviewed prospective employees. She needed to decide how best to communicate what she knew to potential customers. Luckily for Jill and her father, this wasn't the first time she had faced this kind of problem.

As the lead singer and the only female in a heavy-metal rock band in high school, Jill was responsible for getting gigs for her group. She played tapes of her band's performances and got the group auditions.

"But we weren't getting the number of gigs we

should have been getting," Jill said. "I knew we were good, but there were a lot of good bands out there. So I decided we needed to sell ourselves, not just our sound."

Soon Jill began taking the rest of the band along with her when she went to speak to other high schools or clubs.

"People saw how we interacted, how we got along, how much fun we had with each other, and our music," Jill said. "Things got better in a hurry after that."

So the summer of her father's operation, Jill knew what she had to do. She needed to sell herself. She took pictures of the houses the company had shingled in the past. She requested and got written references from happy customers.

"I knew I could demonstrate to prospective customers that my father's company was a good one," Jill said. "That was the easy part. So as they looked at pictures and read customer referrals and recommendations, I talked to them about my role in the company. No numbers or pictures were going to do that for me."

Jill drew on a number of different methods of interpreting and communicating information she learned both as a student bandleader and as a fledgling roofing contractor. She used audio (her band tapes), graphics (the roofing photographs), written communication (customer referrals), and oral presentations (talking to customers about herself).

As Jill's story shows, we've come a long way since the Pleistocene epoch. Most of us no longer communicate with only grunts and pointing. However, even the most educated and worldly people can become daunted by the sheer amount of information now out there. Many of us find ourselves as bewildered by Web pages and software as Pleistocene creatures would have been by an electric shaver.

But while the Pleistocenes could only shake their hairy heads and kill an animal, you already possess many of the information management skills necessary to succeed in the business world of the next century. This book will help you identify the skills you need, hone the skills you have, and develop the skills that will help you now and in the future.

You already possess many of the information management skills necessary to succeed in the business world of the next century.

C H A P T E R T W O

IT'S NO LONGER WHAT YOU KNOW BUT WHAT YOU CAN FIND OUT

Most of us have seen countless images of the stereotypical scientist making discoveries. The scientist is usually a man, working in a dark and dank laboratory, surrounded by test tubes and smoking, bubbling beakers. He has an assistant—either a beautiful and dedicated woman, or a guy who looks like an experiment gone bad—who remains at the scientist's side as he labors for hours and hours, never seeing daylight, never living life outside of the laboratory.

But if this were the only way to acquire information, very little information would ever be acquired. Not too many people want to spend their days trapped in the dark with a man who makes Igor look good. Information is everywhere, and there are a variety of ways to get at it.

There are many ways to obtain information, including observation, interviewing, traditional resources, and

(Joe Duffy)

"Heavens NO! I'm going to need something that holds MUCH more information!"

even actual experience. Before we talk about the latest and most pervasive—the Internet—we'll take a look at the more traditional ways of acquiring information.

OBSERVATION

Young adults are often chastised for hanging out. But hanging out can be a great way of acquiring information.

From 1960–62 the writer Gay Talese hung out. He wanted to write a book on the building of the Verrazano-Narrows Bridge, which was being built to connect Staten Island to Brooklyn, New York. According to the editors of *The Literature of Reality,* Talese "practiced the fine art of 'hanging out.'" For two years Talese hung out near the bridge, watched the workers walking the beams and eating their lunches hundreds of feet in the air.

"I was so regularly in attendance at the bridge in my off-hours and vacations from the *New York Times* that I was practically considered one of the staff of U.S. Steel," Talese said.

An advantage of observation is that it does not require conversation. You can observe pedestrians on a sidewalk 20 stories below or people who do not speak your language.

—Barbara and Robert Sommer,
A Practical Guide to Behavioral Research

(Thomas Monaster)

When you're on a research project, being observant and "hanging out" are traditional methods of acquiring accurate information. Author Gay Talese did just that when writing his book about the construction of the Verrazano-Narrows Bridge in New York in the 1960s.

Even if you're hanging out at the local mall, you could be acquiring information, depending on how much attention you're paying to your surroundings. For instance, just by visiting the mall on a Monday and on a Friday, you could begin to acquire information. Do more people shop on Fridays or Mondays? Are shoppers alone on Monday and with somebody else on Friday? Do more women shop on Monday than on Friday? Do men shop alone?

Now, of course, you couldn't draw too many conclusions or make grand generalizations from just hanging out at the mall for two nights. (Remember, Talese hung out for two years to write *The Bridge.*) But it could be a start to learning more about the shopping habits of mall mavens, if that were indeed your goal.

Hanging out also could lead to another way of acquiring knowledge, and that's through interviews.

INTERVIEWING

Let's say you've come to the conclusion that more women seem to shop alone on Monday nights than on Friday nights. You've been observing this phenomenon at the mall for two weeks and now you want to check the accuracy of your hunch. What do you do?

While Talese hung out at the bridge, he got to know many of the workers. They learned what he was doing. They talked to him almost every day. He earned their trust. Soon he was able to begin interviewing. Because you probably won't have two years to spend on most of your information-gathering projects, you'll have to shorten the process.

If you've been hanging out at the mall for any length of time, you've probably seen some of the same faces night after night. Let's say the manager of the shoe store has smiled at you a time or two. Maybe you've even exchanged greetings. She could be a likely person to interview. You could ask her if she has some time to be interviewed at her convenience. Begin the interview by telling her your name and the purpose of the interview—whether it's a school project or your boss has asked you to find out what would be a good time to set up a display in the mall.

Here's how Andy handled just such an assignment.

For as long as he could remember, Andy had dreamed of becoming a photographer. He took pictures at every family wedding and during each family vacation since he was old enough to hold a camera.

"At my cousin's wedding, I didn't take any pictures of the bride," Andy said. "I was too interested in the people wandering to and from the bar."

Andy's first job out of college was not his dream

job. Instead of having his own studio and being his own boss, Andy had to earn money by working with a studio photographer who specialized in baby pictures. His first assignment was to find out which day of the week women with babies shopped at a local mall.

The photographer had rented space for a temporary studio in a nearby mall for a special one-day promotion, and he wanted to make sure there would be plenty of traffic from moms with babies and toddlers.

"I really didn't know what to do," Andy said. "I didn't think there would be some kind of book on it, so I went to the mall, did some people watching and talked to some store clerks. By the time I was out of there, I felt pretty confident."

Andy was lucky. Not only was he naturally observant, having a photographer's eye, but he also was charming and polite. He interviewed the assistant manager of a sporting goods store who had worked in the mall for almost 10 years. Soon the sporting goods manager took Andy to several other mall employees, including some who worked at stores specializing in children's clothing. Andy asked them when mothers with babies were most likely to shop. Almost everyone he spoke to said that Monday and Tuesday mornings were the big days for moms with small children. He reported that to his boss, who scheduled his display for Monday morning and took more than 100 baby pictures on the day of the event.

"At the time I didn't think much about it," Andy said. "But when I quit my job and set up my own business as a wedding photographer, the first thing I did was interview recently married couples about what they liked and disliked about their wedding photos. I really knew the value of interviewing and how I could be more successful."

An interview is a conversation with a purpose.

> **—W. V. D. Bingham and B. V. Moore,**
> *How to Interview*

Interviewing is a great way of finding out what other people know, and people are almost always a researcher's greatest resource. And yet the more we observe about the people and the "things" in our environment, the more likely we are to see almost everything as a potential source of information. Tina, an L.P.N. in a nursing home, learned this lesson by sitting in a comfortable chair in her great-grand-mother's house

INTERVIEWING TIPS

1. Ask permission first. State your purpose honestly. Establish rapport.

2. Establish a prearranged time and place. Stick to the time limits you state.

3. Putting yourself at ease is the best way to put an interviewee at ease. Use role playing or conduct practice interviews first.

4. Come prepared with a list of questions that you need answered.

5. Begin with "safe" questions. Ask general questions about the interviewee's job or expertise, the spelling of his or her name, etc.

6. Be patient. Give the interviewee time to respond. Let the interviewee fill the silence.

7. Take careful notes. If you use a tape recorder be sure to obtain permission from the interviewee first.

8. Don't be judgmental. Don't ask questions just to confirm what you already believe.

(Continued on page 38)

(Continued from page 37)

9. Try to avoid questions with a "yes" or "no" answer unless it's a survey questionnaire. Open-ended questions encourage more conversation.

10. Don't stare but don't avoid eye contact either.

11. Be aware of body language and cultural and gender differences regarding body language.

12. Do not be afraid to ask the interviewee to repeat a response if you think you might have misunderstood what he or she said.

13. Do not be afraid to ask questions that arise during the course of the interview.

14. Leave open the possibility for a second interview. For example, ask, "If I have any more questions is it okay if I call you?"

15. When you are at home or work typing up your interview notes, do not hesitate to call the interviewee to double-check quotes or facts. The person probably will not mind being called again. He or she will mind being misquoted.

She looked around her great-grandmother's dining room and noticed things she didn't remember seeing before. A framed poster hung on the wall above her great-grandmother's oak hutch. In it a young man appears to be drowning. His eyes are wide open and his mouth is stretched as if screaming. He reaches out of the water, as if extending a hopeful but desperate hand to the viewer. Behind him a ship sinks into a storm-racked ocean. Beneath him is a caption, reading, "Loose lips sink ships."

Tina recognized the caption as something Americans at home were told during World War II as a warning not to divulge information that might be useful to the enemy.

"As I looked at the poster, I couldn't help wondering about some of my patients in the nursing home. What did they go through in their lives before they got here?" Tina said. "I was only on the job for a year and I was already kind of bored and thinking I had nothing to learn from my patients. I thought differently after that. I started asking some of them about what they remembered most about World War II. Some of them really opened up and told me some fascinating stories. Talking about their experiences really lifted their spirits and it kept me from being bored. I think I'm a better nurse now."

F A C T O I D :

Empiricism is a 17th-century British theory stating that all knowledge is derived from sensory experience, by observation and experimentation.

A library search using reference works can be the best way of seeing the whole and the parts.

TRADITIONAL RESOURCES

Generally, the best place to begin any research project is in the library. Although as we have said, there is a glut of information available, a library search using reference works can be the best way of seeing the whole and the parts. For example, if you're interested in the Roman Empire, an encyclopedia will present an overview, but also will break down the discussion of the Roman Empire into sections on history, government, labor, etc., which could be the first step in narrowing the focus of your research.

Reference works include encyclopedias, dictionaries, bibliographies, indexes, atlases, handbooks, and almanacs. In no way should your research be confined to these sources. However, they are often a good place to begin. Scanning these sources can help you focus the angle for your research. Also, these reference works will lead you to more specific and detailed sources.

Periodicals, including newspapers, magazines, and journals, also are important resources. Magazines are publications for the general public. They often cover a variety of issues and appeal to a wide range of readers. The advantage of magazines is their timeliness. Most magazines come out weekly or monthly, allowing them to keep up with current trends and events better than books can, while still being able to offer more in-depth coverage than newspapers.

Journals differ from magazines in one fundamental way. They are usually designed and published for a very specialized audience. For instance, *The Journal of American Folklore* has a much smaller and more specialized readership than *People* magazine. This distinction does not make one a more valuable research tool than the other, just different.

But before you begin paging through past issues of hundreds of magazines and newspapers to locate an article on your subject, consult indexes, such as the *Reader's Guide to Periodical Literature* or the *New York Times* Index, to help you locate specific issues and topics.

Books, of course, will be listed in the library's catalog alphabetically by the author's last name, but you also can search by topic or subject.

Many of the indexes (and other research texts) listed above can also be found on CD-ROMs. Many

(V. Harlow/Electrical Associates)

Searching the Internet enables you to access many current sources, including encyclopedias, almanacs, and magazines, and makes it easy to locate information from practically all countries of the world without leaving your desk.

libraries also subscribe to commercial information services that provide reports and the like from publishers and other corporations. These types of services usually charge a fee.

Another excellent source of information is the Educational Resources Information Center (ERIC). ERIC contains indexes, abstracts and, in some cases, publishes the full texts from nearly 1,000 education journals.

Knowledge is of two kinds:
we know a subject ourselves,
or we know where we can find
information about it.

— Samuel Johnson,
English Author

HOW TO EVALUATE
TRADITIONAL SOURCES

You can begin to determine a source's usefulness and relevance to your needs by first scanning the introduction, table of contents, indexes, and headings.

Also, try to answer these questions about the sources you choose:

- Does the source devote attention to your topic?
- Is the source specialized enough to meet your needs? Does it treat topics in too detailed or too superficial a way?
- How current is the source?
- What are the author's credentials?
- What is the author's bias? Read the author's preface or introduction.
- What do other experts say about this book or about this author?

THE INTERNET AND
THE WORLD WIDE WEB

There's no doubt that careful observation, purposeful interviewing, and traditional resources can get you a long way in the information game. Tina and Andy could tell you that.

But we live in a time where we have access to an electronic, global library. At one time in history, people had to travel to Alexandria, Egypt, where the first—and for a time the only—large library in the world was located. Now we need only venture into our homes, schools, or offices.

The *Internet* is the name for the vast collection of interconnected computer networks around the world, which allows users to:

- Access newspapers, electronic books, and journals.
- Search library catalogues from around the world.
- Search a wide variety of databases.
- Seek information from experts.
- Send and receive e-mail from residents of the electronic global village.

The *World Wide Web*—you know, it's the "www" in "www.com"—resides on the Internet. Just as the Internet is a system of interconnected computer networks, the Web is interconnected information.

More than 20,000 newsgroups (interest groups, i.e., people interested in computers, the sciences, etc.) currently exist on the Net.

CONDUCTING A WEB SEARCH

Let's say Tina wanted to find out more about the loose lips and sinking ships of World War II. Here are the initial steps she most likely would have to take:

1. She'd begin by activating her Web browser (such as Navigator, Explorer, or AOL).
2. She'd pick a directory or index and tell her browser to go there.
3. When Tina saw a search box, she'd type in her keywords and click.
4. After she picked a directory or index and told her Web browser to go there, she could then skip number 3 and choose a topic area from a menu. (For example, if Tina went to the search engine called Yahoo! she could pick the education area from the Yahoo! menu, which would lead her to history and then World War II. Even when she gets to WW II, she'll have a great deal of information to sort through before getting to the loose lips and sinking ships.)

Remember, anybody, and I mean anybody, can put something on the Web. This means that even somebody's Aunt Martha who believes she not only fought as a submarine captain in World War II but also lived during the Pleistocene epoch could show up on your Internet search. This is the reason that being able to evaluate information (the subject of Chapter 3) is critical.

MAJOR INTERNET
SEARCH ENGINES

- **AltaVista**   *http://www.altavista.digital.com*
- **Excite**   *http://www.excite.com*
- **Hotbot**   *http://www.hotbot.com*
- **Infoseek**   *http://guide.infoseek.com*
- **Lycos**   *http://www.lycos.com*
- **Webcrawler** *http://www.webcrawler.com*
- **Yahoo!**   *http://www.yahoo.com*

It is the close observation of little things which is the secret of success in business, in art, in science, and in every pursuit of life. Human knowledge is but an accumulation of small facts, made by successive generations... the littlest bits of knowledge and experience carefully treasured up and growing at length into a mighty pyramid.

—Samuel Smiles,
Scottish Biographer

EXERCISE

Choose a topic you are discussing in one of your school classes or that could help you on your part-time job.

Next, take two hours and acquire as much information as you can on that subject using observation, interviewing, and the Internet.

With which method were you most comfortable?

Which helped you the most? Which helped you the least? Why?

FIVE QUESTIONS FOR INFORMATION HUNTERS

1. Where should I begin?
- Observation?
- Interview?
- Internet?

2. Do I know exactly what I'm looking for?
(You may find great information that is of no use to you at a particular time.)

3. How much time do I have?
(Sometimes, you can get the right answer in a big hurry by picking up the telephone and calling your local university, library, or a local expert.)

4. How will I know when I'm through researching?

5. What will I do with the information once I have it?

CHAPTER THREE
HOW TO BECOME A PICKY EATER AT THE INFORMATION BUFFET

Never before has so much information been almost literally at our fingertips. And everybody, or nearly everybody, has access to the same information you do. This makes being able to look at information critically and to evaluate it carefully the skill that could distinguish you from the countless other people who have the World Wide Web in their family rooms and 200 channels on their televisions.

My sources are unreliable, but their
information is fascinating.
>   —Ashleigh Brilliant,
>   "Street" Philosopher,
>   University of California, Berkeley

EVALUATING INFORMATION

Almost every job today requires information evaluation skills. What information is relevant? What information should you believe? What information is out of date? Doctors, lawyers, and business managers have to carefully sift and evaluate information on a daily basis. But the importance of such skills is perhaps most easily seen in a career such as journalism.

Almost every job today requires information evaluation skills.

Megan seemed to have it all. She had been the editor in chief of her high school and her college newspapers. She graduated with an A average and did particularly well in her journalism classes.

By the time Megan was 23 and had been a reporter on a midsize daily newspaper for over a year, she was becoming a little restless for "the big story." Along with all her education and her experience, Megan was also aggressive and ambitious. She never shied away from the hard questions or the tough stories. And yet, she had never quite mastered the ability to evaluate information. She admitted that the thought of getting a big story often clouded her judgment. But this was before "the hospital story," as it's known to Megan and others around the newsroom.

One morning Megan received a phone call from a woman who said she had information about how a local hospital was mistreating its elderly patients. Although the woman wouldn't give Megan her name, she did agree to meet at a restaurant near the newspaper.

The woman Megan met appeared credible. She told story after story about patients being abused by orderlies, nurses and doctors. When Megan asked for names of the patients, the woman told her that they were all afraid to talk to a reporter. All communicating would have to be done through her. Because of the importance of the story and because Megan could understand the trepidation of elderly people who had already been victimized once, she agreed to the woman's conditions.

Megan then arranged interviews with the hospital's media relations spokesperson and several nurses. She was told by everybody that an orderly had been fired five years ago for neglecting patients, but there had been no other incidents at the hospital before or after.

Doubting the hospital's version of its patient care, Megan gained permission to interview current patients. Although some people complained about the food or about having to buzz the nurses several times, Megan realized these were minor complaints.

Megan then checked the public record for any reports filed against the hospital but found nothing particularly horrifying. After several discussions with her editor and her source, Megan dropped the story. The whole newspaper staff had heard rumors of the big story Megan was about to write. Megan had been strutting her stuff and had come up empty.

"I've never been more embarrassed in my life," Megan said. "It's like I had blinders on. Every other source seemed to contradict what this woman was telling me, but I kind of shut everything else out."

Megan was in a difficult position. Reporters are often told things by sources that public relations people deny but that reporters later find to be true. Megan's problem was that she kept amassing a great deal of information, even though nothing corroborated what the woman had told her. She placed the woman's information above every other piece of information out there.

Megan learned the hard way that all information is not created equal.

We all evaluate information every day. If somebody you don't trust—or is always spreading rumors—tells you something, you're probably not going to believe them. If you trust your parents, minister, or boss and one of them tells you you're doing something wrong, you're likely to believe what he or she is saying and take a look at your own behavior.

What Megan didn't know and didn't take the time or effort to find out was that the woman who made the allegations had recently been fired from her cleaning job at the hospital. She refused to give her name because Megan would have discovered that her informant had an ax to grind. And as many reporters know, information coming from a grinding ax is usually exaggerated or just untrue.

The more gross the fraud the more glibly will it go down and the more greedily will it be swallowed, since folly will always find faith wherever inposters will find impudence.
—Christian Nestell Bovee,
American Author

Primary Sources

Whenever possible, you should rely on primary sources. (But as Megan discovered, even primary sources—in this case her own interviews—can be suspect and should be held to intense and thoughtful scrutiny.)

Primary sources are firsthand, generally contem-poraneous accounts, including letters, speeches, historical documents, eyewitness reports, works of literature, firsthand reports on experiments and surveys and, of course, your own observations, interviews, and correspondence.

In a court of law, a letter written the day after an event occurred is almost always regarded as more telling evidence than, say, six months later. The same is true when it comes to historical evidence. A dispatch written by a general from the battlefield has greater credibility than what he says in his memoirs written 20 years later. Why? Because not only do memories fade over time, but 20/20 hindsight leads us to reshape our recollections to fit what happened later or put our own thoughts and actions in a better light.

When you have acquired all of this firsthand, primary information, it will be up to you to evaluate and draw your own conclusions.

Secondary Sources

The next best origins of information are secondary sources. Secondary sources are reports or analyses of information drawn from other (often primary) sources. Secondary sources include: one doctor's evaluation of other doctors' studies, an English professor's reading of a poem, a historian's account of a

False or misleading information can easily be cloaked in euphemisms or fine sundry words as the British writer George Orwell pointed out in his essay on the politics of the English language.

battle, an encyclopedia or any of the other reference works discussed in Chapter 2.

Secondary sources are useful as a way of summarizing events, so that you as a researcher can get a handle on a particular angle or focus.

Euphemisms

Effective information management means not disseminating false information or facts cloaked n euphemisms.

Just as with a book where you will want to read the author's preface and biographical information to make an informed judgment about the information in the book, the same is true of firsthand sources, as Megan learned the hard way. Effective information management means not disseminating false information or facts cloaked (and often hidden) in euphemisms and what the writer George Orwell called the "politics of the English language."

For instance, if somebody in the government releases a statement that there was "collateral damage" during a military operation, you need to be critical and realize that collateral damage means civilian casualties.

The mainstream press swallowed whole the now-famous statement made by President Ronald Reagan regarding the Iran-Contra scandal. Reagan used the passive voice effectively when he said of the scandal, "mistakes were made." This was not information; this

EXERCISE

Answer the following questions "yes" or "no."

To learn about a company you are considering to working for, would you:

• Talk to someone who has worked there for several years?

• Talk to someone who has worked there for a week?

• Check on the company with the Better Business Bureau?

• Look up articles on the company in local newspapers in your library?

• Search the Internet for information on the company?

• Talk to customers?

• Talk to somebody the company fired for stealing?

was what the administration wanted the public to think. Amazingly enough, in 1997 President Bill Clinton repeated the exact same phrase when asked about campaign fund-raising scandals. In politics,

(V. Harlow/Russell Library)

When you start a project and need to learn some basic facts about the subject, a good place to search is the periodical section of your local library. There you will find accurate and current information at your fingertips.

apparently, people don't make mistakes, the mistakes make themselves. Even reputable sources have their own agendas to which you as an acquirer of information must be alert.

Hear one side and you will be in the dark:
hear both sides, and all will be clear.
> —Thomas Haliburton,
> Nova Scotian Humorist

INFORMATION OVERLOAD

In this day and age, more often we have too much rather than too little information. Information overload can easily paralyze our ability to make decisions. In most situations, it's simply impossible to pull together all the information available on a subject. We need to focus on the essential information, as Brendan's case illustrates.

Just after graduating from college, Brendan accepted a job for the National Park Service. His dream was to work with fledgling wolf populations. Whenever he talked with his friends about wolves, they all seemed interested, but nobody else was considering making a living working with wolves.

He set out to learn all he could about the reintroduction of wolves into parts of the northwestern United States. During his first year of employment with the Park Service, Brendan had received positive evaluations from his superiors and made some national connections. Now he had to learn about the wolves of the Rocky Mountains.

Drawing on his experiences from high school and college, Brendan knew enough to begin his search with periodicals in the library. He read all he could about recent reintroductions of wolves in Canada. He wrote down every name mentioned in the article and every source quoted. He was on his way.

And then he got in trouble.

"All of a sudden I felt overwhelmed," Brendan said. "I thought finding out about the reintroduction would be easy. I mean it was a one-time thing, and it just happened. Pretty soon it felt like I had to know everything about everything."

Brendan was faced with an ordinary, yet daunting dilemma: How much information was enough? How much was too much?

Everybody gets so much information all day long that they lose their common sense.
— **Gertrude Stein (1874–1946),**
American writer

He soon learned that to talk intelligently about the wolves of the Rocky Mountain region, he needed to find out not only what just happened, but what had happened some 60 years ago, when thousands of wolves were systematically eliminated from the Rocky

Thanks to modern technology, we have so much information available to us that it's easy to become overwhelmed. Stay focused on the subject and only collect the facts that are directly relevant to your search. American writer, Gertrude Stein, warned of the dangers of information overload nearly 100 years ago.

Mountain region of the United States. Brendan also decided he should research ranching practices in the region because ranchers were the most vocal opponents of the wolf reintroduction.

Soon Brendan was on the Internet. He learned about wolf reintroduction in parts of Canada and about wolf populations in other parts of the world, including Italy, Russia, and Israel, now and in the past. At that point Brendan began to feel overwhelmed by all he didn't know and all there was to know about wolves around the world.

Then it clicked. His goal was to learn enough about the reintroduction of wolves to Yellowstone National Park so that he could transfer within the Park Service. He didn't have to become the world's greatest expert on wolves.

He made files for wolf populations around the world and stored that information for future use. Brendan threw out studies on the specific ways that wolf mythology paralleled beliefs held by some modern practitioners of witchcraft. Not that he wasn't interested, but now he understood the value of remaining focused when feasting at the information buffet.

Brendon focused on finding out the specifics of the most recent Yellowstone reintroduction, including the reaction of the local ranchers.

(V. Harlow/Russell Library)

Your local library is a great resource when searching for information on almost any subject. Don't overlook consumer files, various indexes, vertical files, or special collections, which may house precisely the facts you need for your research.

The most important thing you can do to avoid crumbling under the weight of information is to know what you're looking for. Brendan forgot what the focus of his search was, so he was vulnerable to any and all information. While your stamina will inform you when it is time to stop interviewing, young adults usually run into trouble with information overload when it comes to library research.

There's a curious thing about information overload: when people feel there's just too much information and they cannot seem to get a handle on all of it, they end up with no information at all or at least not any useful information.

To ensure you remain focused and avoid information overload caused by poor organization or a weak research strategy:

1. Know your research task thoroughly.
2. Keep a working bibliography and/or take notes.
3. Get an overview of your subject first. This means beginning with the reference sources as a way of finding your focus. (Check encyclopedias, subject headings in books, bibliographies.)
4. Locate your sources. (Check books, periodicals, newspapers, government reports, and statistical sources.) When you are deciding which books to use, check the index first. If the book devotes only a page or two to your topic, it's probably not the right book for you. A good rule of thumb is this: if it's not listed in the index, it's not in the book.
5. Choose and read sources with a critical eye, for relevance and for bias.

EXERCISE

Think of a general topic (like Brendan's topic of wolves in the Rockies). Define a specific goal for your search. Now ask yourself all the places your search could lead you.

Which information would you use?

Which might you store for the future?

Which would you be better off throwing away?

6. When conducting a computer search (either CD-ROM or the World Wide Web), select your keywords carefully. Make sure your keywords are as precise and as accurate as possible. This will help ensure that your search results in a manageable list of sites. When your computer search results in 395,000 sources relevant to your topic, you had better come up with more precise keywords before initiating a new search strategy.

When you think you have done all your research and still feel that there might be something you have missed, do not panic. First, take a deep breath, and then check these often overlooked sources:

1. *Vertical files:* Pamphlets and brochures from government and private agencies.
2. *Special collections:* Manuscripts and rare books.
3. *Audio collections:* Records, audiocassettes, music, readings, speeches, CD-ROMs.
4. *Video collections:* Slides, filmstrips, videocassettes.
5. *Art collections:* Drawings and paintings.

CHAPTER FOUR
NOW WHAT DO I DO WITH IT?

You have read about acquiring information and how you have been doing it all of your life. We've talked about observation and interviewing, and you have gotten a few tips and have read a couple of stories about evaluating information. This chapter takes us into the area of organizing and maintaining the information you do acquire.

Although we have treated these facets of information separately, it's likely that when you're in the workforce full-time, you'll be performing all of these tasks nearly simultaneously.

In many instances, employees find themselves having to organize text (both on paper and on computer) and numbers (usually in the form of graphs, tables, spreadsheets, or databases).

(Joe Duffy)

"When you're through, don't forget to make a copy on this 'back up' disc."

ORGANIZING INFORMATION

Some philosophers have speculated that human beings have a natural urge to organize their environments. Perhaps it's a way of deluding ourselves into believing we can control the universe in a small way if we have our underwear and socks separate from our swimsuits, and our T-shirts in a different drawer than our jeans. Maybe it's a way to stave off chaos.

Even the Pleistocene man in Chapter 1 must have had a way of organizing the spoils of his daily hunt. Surely he separated the meat from the skin and the bones from the teeth. Maybe his subconscious— which he, of course, did not even know he had—let him feel a sense of control over the chaos, or maybe it just made sense to put what he planned to eat in one corner of the cave and what he planned to make tools out of in a different corner.

And again, just as you have been acquiring information most of your life, you've also been organizing information, which probably began by keeping your stuffed animals away from your Hot Wheels.

But one of the tricks is learning how to organize the information that you're still gathering.

Deleasa works as an assistant in a job placement firm. Her boss began the company with the sole purpose of matching top-level executives and management personnel with high-tech firms. However, the company soon decided it had better diversify.

"It was the old cliché about not putting all your eggs in one basket," Deleasa said.

Soon Deleasa found herself inundated with resumés from blue-collar and service technician job seekers as well as executives.

"Everybody in the firm was already overworked," Deleasa said. "I knew I had to do something myself and do it quickly or I'd be buried beneath tons of paper. I call it the landfill effect."

FACTOID:

A database is nothing more than an assortment of related information that is systematically organized in some way.

Deleasa already had a solid database set up for people seeking executive and managerial jobs. She continued to input new information into the database she already had. Deleasa also needed to create a database for people seeking service and technical jobs. And, in the meantime, she also had to organize the new flood of paper arriving on her desk into files until she had the time to create another computer database.

(V. Harlow)

Transferring your research notes from paper files to a computer database can help you retain and retrieve information quickly. It also saves office space and keeps your projects up-to-date and organized.

Deleasa quickly got her hands on as many file folders as she could, and she labeled them simply according to jobs the company sought to fill. For example, she had a folder for electricians and another file for people looking for jobs in computer repair. Then separate subcategories emerged. All the folders containing electricians who also had college degrees went together, separate from those without degrees.

Before she knew it, Deleasa was not only keeping up with her daily entries into the existing computer databases, but she was also organizing the "paper" database by simply slipping an incoming resumé into the proper folder. She then asked her boss if she could work overtime on Saturday in order to transfer her paper files into the computer.

"I panicked for a little while," Deleasa said. "And then I just relied on what I had at my disposal. Common sense and a stack of file folders. If I'd tried to create a database and input everything as it came in, it would have been a mess. I wouldn't have known how to structure it and might have to redo it two or three times. I might have freaked out and given up. Then where would I be?"

Organization most often begins by putting like items with like items. When you first put all your toys with wheels in one box and all those without in another box, you were beginning to learn how to organize. As early as grade school, you probably had one notebook and folder for your science class and another for your English class.

The first thing you need to do when organizing any information is determine the major categories. Make sure the categories are inclusive, that all your material will fit into one of your selected categories.

Next, divide the material you need to organize into the separate, inclusive categories you have chosen. Then, see if you need subcategories. Make ongoing adjustments to your organizational strategy when necessary. For example, if you need to add a category, add one. If you need to divide one inclusive category into two, do so. Then have faith in your system.

The first thing you need to do when organizing any information is determine the major categories.

For years the staple of the office environment has been the filing cabinet. Documents were stored in filing folders, usually alphabetically. Often, one drawer of the filing cabinet would contain invoices while another held work orders. As companies expanded and evolved, files were stored by years, and then alphabetically by invoices, work orders, etc.

If you look at just about anything, you will notice the layers of organization, like putting your English essays on one side of the folder and your English exams on the other. Even with the advent of computer storage, laser discs, and videocassettes, these same fundamental organizational principles apply: organization within organization.

For example, everyone who uses a computer soon learns that you have to organize the information on your hard drive into logical "directories" and "subdirectories" within directories. Otherwise, you soon won't be able to find and retrieve anything you've saved on your hard drive. A computer's hard drive is very similar to an old-fashioned file cabinet with draws (directories) containing file folders (subdirectories) in which you file paper (electronic files).

EXERCISE

Were there other ways Deleasa could have organized the information? How would you have done it? Was there a downside to what Deleasa did?

Take a few minutes to think this through and then write a brief response.

SPREADSHEETS

In Chapter 1 you read about Chris the second-year stockbroker. Chris sat in a meeting with a smile on his face when his managers spoke to him and other employees about the benefits and uses of spread-sheets. Chris had used spreadsheets before he even knew that's what they were called to track the value of his baseball card collection.

A spreadsheet is a grid of "cells" formed by rows and columns. Each cell can contain a number or a mathe-matical formula, and the contents of any one cell can be added to, subtracted from, divided by, or multiplied by the contents of any other cell in the spreadsheet. Best of all, any time you change the contents of one cell, all the other cells linked to it will change accordingly! That makes repetitive, difficult and complex calculations— that could take hours to perform using a calculator—a snap. Indeed, they happen instantaneously and, if you've set up and tested the spreadsheet correctly, without ever making a mistake.

For example, let's say you need to begin budgeting your money. You know you have monthly expenses and a fixed income.

Here is where a spreadsheet comes in handy. Down the left hand side column, you list your projected expenses: car, insurance, clothes, entertainment, etc.

(V. Harlow)

A spreadsheet can help you perform a variety of complex calculations whether you're tracking invoices or bills, budgeting your monthly expenses, or doing more advanced accounting. Utilizing a spreadsheet rather than working on a calculator saves time and also stores the information so that you can access it easily in the future.

Along the top row, list the months of the year. Then at a glance, you'll be able to calculate how much money you'll need on hand in any particular month.

So far, here's what your spreadsheet looks like:

SPREADSHEET 1

	A	B	C	D	E	F	G
		Jan.	Feb.	Mar.	Apr.	May	June
1	Take-home pay						
2	Savings						
3	Car						
4	Insurance						
5	Clothes						
6	Total essential expenses						
7	Net (take-home minus expenses) left for gas, entertainment						

Computer spreadsheet programs, like Lotus, do all kinds of sophisticated calculations for you. By changing one number, the program makes the necessary calculations. This is what enables spreadsheets to work out "what-if" scenarios.

For example, let's say your monthly take-home pay is $700. You need to save $150 a month for college tuition, your monthly car payment is $135, you have quarterly insurance payments of $200 and you typically spend $50 a month on new clothes. These you regard as your essential expenses—and note that we put savings first. Whatever's left over you would like to spend on gas and entertainment. You plug these numbers in the first month of your spreadsheet, and it looks like this.

SPREADSHEET 2

	A	B	C	D	E	F	G
		Jan.	Feb.	Mar.	Apr.	May	June
1	Take-home pay	$700					
2	Savings	$150					
3	Car	$135					
4	Insurance	$200					
5	Clothes	$50					
6	Total essential expenses						
7	Net (take-home minus expenses) left for gas, entertainment						

The spreadsheet lets you copy numbers across rows. So, now you copy across the numbers in rows 1, 2, 3, and 5 because they should be the same every month. You didn't copy the $200 for car insurance across because you only pay that once every three months, so you put $200 in cell E4. Now you want to add up your essential expenses for each month by putting a simple formula in cell B6 that would look like this SUM@(B2..B5). In other words, you tell the computer to add up all four cells in column B between rows 2 and 5 and put them here. Now, when you copy that formula across row 6, the machine is smart enough to know that you don't want to keep putting the sum of the cells in column B in each of them; instead it changes the formula to apply to that column. So it puts the formula SUM@(C2..C5) in cell C6, the formula SUM@ (D2..D5) in cell D6, etc. Now your spreadsheet looks like the illustration on the next page labeled "Spreadsheet 3".

Now it's time to put in a formula that will tell you what you have available for "discretionary spending," otherwise known as entertainment to many people. To do so, you put a formula (B1 – B6) in cell B7. In other words, you tell the computer to subtract your total essential expenses from your take-home pay so

	SPREADSHEET 3					
A	**B**	**C**	**D**	**E**	**F**	**G**
	Jan.	Feb.	Mar.	Apr.	May	June
1 Take-home pay	$700	$700	$700	$700	$700	$700
2 Savings	$150	$150	$150	$150	$150	$150
3 Car	$135	$135	$135	$135	$135	$135
4 Insurance	$200	$0	$0	$200	$0	$0
5 Clothes	$50	$50	$50	$50	$50	$50
6 Total essential expenses	$535	$335	$335	$535	$335	$335
7 Net (take-home minus expenses) left for gas, entertainment						

you see what you can afford on entertainment each month. See spreadsheet 4 on the opposite page.

Looks like it's going to be a squeeze in January and April when you have to make those insurance payments. As a result perhaps you decide to hold down your gas and entertainment to $300 in the other four months and sock the extra $65 away to help you make those quarterly insurance payments and allow you to spend an even amount on gas and entertain-

	A	B	C	D	E	F	G
		Jan.	Feb.	Mar.	Apr.	May	June
1	Take-home pay	$700	$700	$700	$700	$700	$700
2	Savings	$150	$150	$150	$150	$150	$150
3	Car	$135	$135	$135	$135	$135	$135
4	Insurance	$200	$0	$0	$200	$0	$0
5	Clothes	$50	$50	$50	$50	$50	$50
6	Total essential expenses	$535	$335	$335	$535	$335	$335
7	Net (take-home minus expenses) left for gas, entertainment	$165	$365	$365	$165	$365	$365

ment (about $298) every month.

Now suppose—surprise, surprise—"what if" your boss gets generous in March and gives you a salary increase that raises your take-home pay by $50 a month! With a spreadsheet you just change your take-home-pay line and the computer adjusts all the other lines and (remember those formulas) calculates the rest automatically. Your spreadsheet now looks like this and you're in clover:

SPREADSHEET 5

	A	B	C	D	E	F	G
		Jan.	Feb.	Mar.	Apr.	May	June
1	Take-home pay	$700	$700	$750	$750	$750	$750
2	Savings	$150	$150	$150	$150	$150	$150
3	Car	$135	$135	$135	$135	$135	$135
4	Insurance	$200	$0	$0	$200	$0	$0
5	Clothes	$50	$50	$50	$50	$50	$50
6	Total essential expenses	$535	$335	$335	$535	$335	$335
7	Net (take-home minus expenses) left for gas, entertainment	$165	$365	$415	$215	$415	$415

EXERCISE

Make a list of five things you do now with a calculator that you could do better with a spreadsheet.

THINGS YOU CAN DO WITH A SPREADSHEET

▶ Financial planning (the car loan)

▶ Analyzing statistics (Chris's baseball card collection when he was a kid, stock prices now)

▶ Invoices and bills

▶ Budgeting

▶ What-if scenarios

DATABASES

A database is really nothing more than a way of organizing a collection of information.

If you've ever used a library card index, a Rolodex, a dictionary, or a phone book, you've used a database.

> —**David C. Kay,**
> *Microsoft Works 3 for*
> *Windows for Dummies*

A database really proves its worth, however, when you want to take a card index, rolodex, dictionary, or phone book and organize it yet again. *Microsoft Works 3 for Windows for Dummies* provides a good example. Let's say you have 100 people in your Rolodex. A computer database would allow you—in a matter of seconds—to further organize your friends and business associates by zip code or street. If you were planning a wedding or a reunion, using a computer database would allow you to find out immediately how many people in your Rolodex, for instance, live in your state, how many in your zip code, and even who has kids, or any other category of information you have recorded.

Information is stored in a database using fields and records. In a computer database, the rolodex card is called a "record." Just as each card in your Rolodex has spaces for names, addresses and phone numbers, each record in your database has spaces called "fields" (address field, phone number field, etc.). In most database programs, there is almost an unlimited number of records and you can have as many fields as you want. Each field has a different content, just as each card in your Rolodex has different information.

How to find information in a database varies according to which computer and computer software you use.

WORD PROCESSING AND DOCUMENT MANAGEMENT

In the past two decades, the typewriter has been replaced by the desktop computer in almost every office. Word-processing software drove the typewriter into extinction. Why? Because using word-processing software on a desktop computer does everything a typewriter used to do better. It can also do many things a typewriter can't, including:

- Check for and correct misspellings.
- Merge a list of names, addresses, and key information with the text of a letter and personalize every letter. (This is called "mail merge.")
- Cut and paste blocks of text within one document or from one document to another.
- Find and replace one word or phrase with another word or phrase.
- Instantly change the format of a document and the size of the type to fit the page.
- Generate tables of contents and indexes automatically.
- Insert pictures and graphs into a document.
- Format text into columns.
- Use a variety of different typefaces and sizes in the same document.

These capabilities alone probably would have sealed the typewriter's doom, but word-processing programs enable us to do something even more important—because they store documents in digital form, they enable us to *manage documents.* We can save them, retrieve them, modify them, copy them or transmit them around the world without ever leaving our desk.

What does this mean to you? If you already haven't learned the basics of using a word processor, do so as soon as you can. Word processing has become so universal in American businesses that you'll need at least basic word-processing skills in almost any office job. And don't think that word processing is just for secretaries; increasingly companies are expecting managers and professional workers to keyboard their own documents. So much so, that the traditional secretary/typist will soon be as extinct as the typewriter. Don't worry too much about which program you learn. If you learn Microsoft Word, you'll be able to pick up WordPerfect or one of the other popular programs very quickly. And vice versa.

PLAGIARISM
Earlier in this chapter you may have noted that I cited David C. Kay's *Microsoft Works 3 for Windows for Dum-*

WHEN TO USE SPREADSHEETS, DATABASES OR WORD-PROCESSING SOFTWARE

	Spreadsheets	Databases	Word Processing
Budget monthly or weekly expenses	X		
Track addresses of friends and family		X	
Keep track of savings and checking accounts	X		
Cut and paste text from one document to another			X
Keep track of credit card charges	X		
Keep track of phone numbers		X	
Future financial planning	X		
Keeping a parts inventory or price list		X	
Writing term papers			X
Setting up a library card catalog		X	
Tracking bills or invoices	X		
Saving letters or papers electronically			X
Track values of baseball cards, rare records, antiques, etc.	X		
Maintaining and using a set of form letters		X	X
Names, addresses, phone numbers of potential customers		X	

mies. Although I could have created my own example using a "little black book" instead of a Rolodex, I used this particular example because it was convenient and because it worked. But because I used Kay's example, however, he must get the credit.

COPYRIGHT

Copyright law is far too complex to even summarize it here, but the basic principle is fairly simple. If you quote some other writer's work extensively and the writer's work is under copyright protection, you must get permission first if you are creating a work of your own that will be sold for money, such as a book, magazine article, or TV script.

What does the word "extensively" mean in this context? Well, it depends on what percentage of the original text you quote, what percentage it will be of the work you are creating, and what your purpose is. Does that mean if you quote some writer's book in a memo you're writing to your boss, you need to get permission? No. But if you were writing a company employee handbook you probably would.

It is a poor wit who lives by borrowing the words, decisions, miens, inventions, and actions of others.

—John Lavater,
Swiss Theologian

EXERCISE

Say you were going to use each of the following in a school paper. Which ones could raise questions about plagiarism?

1. "To be or not to be, that is the question."

2. The earth revolves around the sun.

3. In Australia, 33% of all aboriginal tribesmen accumulate six ounces of ear wax every five months.

4. Two paragraphs of information downloaded from a Web page.

5. Chapter 3 of this book.

Only number 2 is safe from any charge of plagiarism. Number 1 is, of course, a quote from Shakespeare, and should be attributed to him even though practically everyone knows it comes from *Hamlet.* Number 3 is obviously such specific information that the researcher who uncovered this fact deserves credit. As far as number 4 is concerned, just because something is found on the Internet doesn't mean you should "borrow" it without giving credit where it's due. Number 5 would be brazen plagiarism.

PLAGIARISM CHECKLIST

1. What types of sources have you used? Your own independent research? Common knowledge? Someone else's material? You must acknowledge it if it is somebody else's material.

2. If you are quoting somebody else's work, is the quotation exact? Have you demonstrated omissions with ellipses or brackets?

3. When paraphrasing or summarizing, have you used your own sentence structure and words? Have you represented the author's words truly?

4. Are uses of somebody else's material acknowledged in your text?

5. Does your bibliography or works cited page include all the sources you have drawn on in your work?

▼

Any time you use another writer's words or even a close paraphrase of his or her words, you must give that writer credit.

Any time you use another writer's words or even a close paraphrase of his or her words, you must give that writer credit. If you don't, you've committed the crime of plagiarism. Simply put, plagiarism is using somebody else's words and claiming or pretending they're your own words. A simple rule of thumb for avoiding plagiarism is: when in doubt, give the writer credit.

If it's common information, you do not have to worry about plagiarism. If you say the earth is round, nobody will accuse you of plagiarism. On the other hand, if you write in a research paper stating that 16.5% of all merchant marines get seasick, chances are some poor researcher spent months of his life to determine that fact. The researcher deserves the credit.

Borrowed thoughts, like borrowed money, only show the poverty of the borrower.
—Lady Blessington, English Author

PAPER FILES AND COMPUTER STORAGE

As you probably already have observed, more schools and businesses are becoming increasingly dependent on computer storage. The days of having rooms set aside merely to store boxes and boxes of dusty documents are gradually coming to an end.

The days of having rooms set aside merely to store boxes and boxes of dusty documents are gradually coming to an end.

Office space is expensive. Corporate executives are realizing that because of technology—particularly the computer chip—one employee working at home can do just as much (if not more) in his or her own home than at the office. Companies can be comprised of several people working in their own homes, sending e-mail and memos and faxing invoices and price sheets. Even if they all work in the same building, how can they all have access to the same data? In other words, where can all the files be stored so that everyone has quick access to them and in a way that doesn't take up a lot of physical space?

The answer, of course, is computer storage.

_____

We're hooked on paper. Tearing it away from workers is like taking heroin away from an addict.

—Technology Inc.

Dan Caulfield, founder of Hire Quality, Inc., had an idea. He knew that money and time were being wasted on paper. He knew what he had to do.

According to *Technology Inc.* magazine, one day Caulfield "stormed through...[the office] with a large metal waste barrel in tow." Caulfield "...gathered every piece of paper he could find...[he then] dragged the barrel out to the fire escape. Before an aghast crowd huddled on the narrow metal stairwell, he doused the trash heap with lighter fluid and set it ablaze."

Caulfield admits that a bonfire on the fire escape was a bit unorthodox, but he felt it had to be done. He is not alone. More and more businesses seek a

(V. Harlow)

Since office space is valuable and often expensive, many businesses and schools are converting from paper files to computer storage because it is more efficient and saves space.

paperless office. Some are turning to more computer storage. Still others are beginning to store information on CD-ROM, optical disks, and client servers.

If there's one prediction about the future that's a safe bet, it's that storing and retrieving information in an electronic form will keep getting cheaper and more convenient. In most offices, paper files may never be completely eliminated, but their importance will diminish compared to electronic records.

EXERCISE

Do you see opportunities at your part-time job to limit the use of paper files and storage? Is there information around the office that could be stored on computers? Do a quick study and write a memo that could be presented to your boss.

Be sure to include cost savings (paper, employee hours, etc.). Also make sure to mention any disadvantages of computer storage. For instance, how would you guard against losing company files if a computer or computer network became infected or crashed?

CHAPTER FIVE

HOW DO I GET ALL THAT INFORMATION INTO A TWO-PAGE MEMO OR A FIVE-MINUTE PRESENTATION?

Remember Brendan, the Park Service ranger, who ran into trouble in his search for information on the wolf population of the Rocky Mountains when he lost sight of his goal. Like a boat cut loose from its moorings, Brendan found himself adrift, carried in whatever direction the tides happened to be going. Something very similar can happen even after you have evaluated and interpreted the information. It's easy to flounder about in a sea of information when it comes time to present to others the information you have acquired, evaluated, and interpreted.

Effective presentations are attention-getting, meaningful, memorable, activating, and balanced. Furthermore, a business presentation is most effective when it satisfies the purpose of presenting, which is to persuade.

—Lani Arredondo,
Business Presentations

Trying to cram in everything will just confuse your listeners by distracting them from the "big picture."

ORAL PRESENTATIONS

Let's say you have spent a month acquiring information about a topic your boss wants you to share with senior management in a five-minute presentation. You now know so much that you can't imagine how you're going to fit it all into a short presentation. The first thing to plant firmly in your mind is that you are not going to fit all you know into that five-minute presentation. Senior management won't want to hear all the details, and trying to cram in everything will just confuse your listeners by distracting them from the "big picture."

Remember, the information you leave out of your presentation is not going anywhere. You'll have it if anyone asks for it. Besides, you will look good if you answer more specific questions about your topic after your presentation, when the questions inevitably start being asked.

Let's bring back Andy (from Chapter 2) for a

minute. If you recall, Andy had to hang out at the mall to find out when mothers with babies shopped. Assuming Andy's boss was a busy photographer, he probably would not have a couple of hours for Andy to tell him all he learned at the mall. As a matter of fact, let's say Andy's boss happens to be in-between shoots. It's Andy's first big assignment, and he has three minutes to present his information to his boss.

Andy's boss will not want to hear about:
- the price of the new Smashing Pumpkins' CD;
- the fact that the young woman behind the jewelry counter smiled at Andy;
- that senior citizens walk around the mall's perimeter for exercise; or
- when women with babies do not shop at the mall.

It is not that this information is inherently less valuable. If Andy's boss wanted to sell pictures of senior citizens, the fact that they could be found at the mall at certain times would be of utmost importance. But he doesn't. The photographer wants to know when mothers with babies shop at the mall. The goal will determine the focus of the presentation.

The first thing Andy should do is summarize the information he has acquired. He'll be able to do this if he first remembers what the point of the exercise was.

97

(V. Harlow)

When trying to acquire information for a project or presentation, stay focused on the goal. If you are interested in finding out about the shopping habits of mothers with small children, concentrate on that and skip other interesting but irrelevant events that will distract you from your objective.

NARROWING THE SCOPE

Andy must first narrow the scope of his material. He cannot possibly tell his boss everything he saw, heard and learned at the mall. If he loses focus and begins talking about the popcorn that got stuck in his teeth on his second afternoon at the mall, his three minutes will be over and his boss will know nothing except that perhaps he needs somebody a little more professional than Andy.

In order to narrow his scope Andy must pick the two, three, or four most important points his boss needs to know in order to decide when to set up shop in the mall.

ORGANIZING THE MATERIAL

The next thing Andy must do is organize his material. He will have no time to ramble. The fact that he has only three minutes makes organizing his presentation even more important.

A good presentation, regardless of the length, has three major components: The introduction, body, and conclusion.

Introduction

The introduction should generally accomplish four basic things:

1. Grab audience's attention.
2. State the basic topic of the presentation.
3. Connect the topic to the audience.
4. Preview the main points of the body.

Body

The body is usually the meat of your presentation. It includes detail and supporting material. Depending, of course, on the length of the body, it should be divided into three or four sections or main points.

- *Main Point #1.* This is your first area of information and is probably your most important point. It should be explained and supported by details.
- *Main Point #2.* This is the second area of information and should also be supported by details.
- *Main Point #3.* This is the third point of information and should be supported in ways similar to points 1 and 2.

This looks simple for a simple reason: it is. The difficult part is determining the main points of your presentation. What is the most important piece of information in all the books, articles, observations, interviews, Web pages, and Internet sites you have acquired?

Conclusion

The conclusion should accomplish two things:

1. It should review the main points of your presentation.
2. It should provide closure and an ending.

TEN THINGS THAT ARE SURE TO KILL ANY PRESENTATION

1. Reading from a paper instead of performing a presentation. (Speak from a "keyword" outline on note cards. You should be familiar enough with the material to do this.)

2. Talking at or over your audience. (People hate to be lectured to.)

3. Avoiding eye contact.

4. Ignoring raised hands or interruptions. (Try to see the unexpected as an opportunity.)

5. Not being prepared.

6. Saying anything considered to be in poor taste.

7. Using discriminatory language.

8. Using "apologetic" language. (Nobody likes a whiner.)

9. Using abbreviations.

10. Using "I" this, and "I" that.

(Joe Duffy)

"I KNOW I had my presentation slides when I left the house this morning."

> **EXERCISE**
>
> Assume you are Andy and have three minutes to present the information he acquired at the mall. Using information you invent, and remembering his goal (to find out when mothers with babies are most likely to shop), write an introduction. Fill in the three main points of the body and provide a conclusion.

MEMO WRITING

No matter what the medium of communication, you need to structure and manage the contents into a beginning, a middle, and an end. Let's say we try to apply what we learned about oral presentations to what has become the most ordinary means of communication: the phone call. Even the ordinary phone call has an introduction: "hello." What follows the agreed-upon introduction is the body of the phone call. The body, not coincidentally, is the purpose for the call. And the conclusion: "thanks for calling," or "thanks for taking my call," or "goodbye."

Written communication, too, has beginnings, middles, and ends. Memos are no exception.

The beginning of any piece of writing has one job, which is to get the reader to read further. If the first chapter of a novel is dull, the reader will close the book. If the first paragraph of a newspaper story (called the "lead") doesn't capture the reader's attention, the reader will likely turn the page to find a story that does. (In inverted pyramid news articles, the entire story is summarized in the lead, usually in fewer than 30 words. Thus, if the reader only reads the first paragraph, he or she will know the who, what, where, why, when, and how of any given story.)

People do not read every piece of writing they're handed. If they did, those guys passing out pamphlets on street corners would have it a lot easier.

If your boss requests a memo on a certain topic or event, you will have a reader whether you want one or not. One good rule of thumb is this: If the reader (your boss, for instance) is expecting the memo, begin the memo with a summary of its content. If the reader is not expecting the memo, begin with something that will make sure the person reads the memo.

Most memos:
- Communicate the data in narrative form.
- Are accompanied by a table or graph if the narrative text includes a lot of numerical data. (Tables and graphs are discussed in detail in Chapter 6.)
- Have subheads for each section and subsection.
- Have subheads that are informative.

CHAPTER SIX

6 MAKE THE PRESENTATION FIT THE DATA

As the previous chapter has shown, you can be on your way to giving an effective presentation by getting prepared, remaining focused, and being organized, whether it is a written memo or an oral report.

Still, you can be the most organized, focused, and prepared presenter, and your presentation can still fail. It is not only what you communicate, but the tools you use. Some information can best be presented in a narrative form. Other kinds of information, such as quantitative data, are best presented in graphic form.

INFOGRAPHICS (INFORMATIONAL GRAPHICS)

By now you've heard the old adage, "Seeing is believing." You're also intelligent enough to know that you cannot always believe everything you see, read, hear, think, or feel. But there are still times—and presentations are one of them—when visual aids can help you organize your information in such a way that people can grasp it. The following sections describe the most common infographics.

Bar Graphs

Bar graphs are perhaps the most commonly used chart. Their real value is in demonstrating that something is bigger than something else. For example, suppose you work for a consumer products company that makes bath soap. You have been assigned the task of speaking to the local chapter of the Sierra Club about how much less paper your company uses now compared to five years ago.

You could, for instance, create a bar graph with two or three trees. The smallest tree becomes a symbol for how much less paper you use. The huge tree at the far left of the bar graph shows how much paper your company used five years ago.

Be aware that a bar graph with more than three bars can become cumbersome and complicate your goal.

Line Graphs

Just as bar graphs are most effective at showing comparisons, line graphs are most effective at showing change over time. For instance, they can be used to

Bar Graph

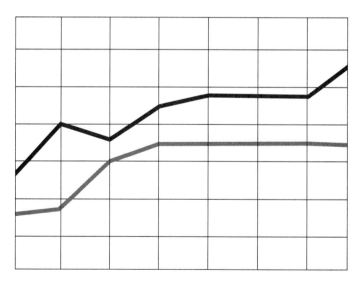

Line Graph

show salary trends of employees who know how to give effective presentations versus those who do not. Line graphs work best when you have many observations over a period of time.

Pie Chart

Pie charts are used almost exclusively to show the totality of something sliced up into parts. For example, if you wanted to show what sports the members of your debate team prefer to watch on television, a pie chart would be an effective tool.

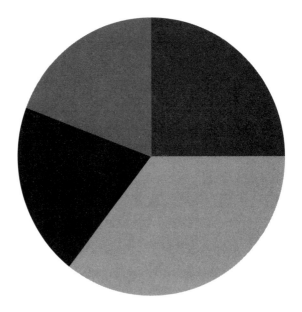

Pie Chart

108

By slicing up the pie, you could show that 35% prefer football; 25% basketball; 20% baseball; and 20% other sports.

CREATING AND PRESENTING INFOGRAPHICS

Here are some tips on creating and presenting high quality, effective infographics:

- The function of an infographic is to convey information in a visual form.
- Just like the memo, and oral presentations, infographics also have a beginning, a middle, and an end.
- Make sure your graphic has an easy-to-read headline.
- Make sure your graphic has an "explainer" beneath the headline. An explainer consists of a few words explaining the graphic and why the information presented is important. (Caution: The explainer should add to the information in the graphic rather than simply restating it.)
- The body of the infographic is the data presented graphically. Besides the line graphs, bar graphs, and pie charts we have covered, the data in an infographic also can be a map or

(Courtesy: David Letterman)

The use of infographics is one effective way to present information in a visual form. The use of infographics in newspapers has become so widespread that **Late Show** *host David Letterman cracks jokes about it.*

drawing. *USA Today* has set the standard in the newspaper business for its use of info-graphics.

- The infographic should have a source listed at the bottom, which informs the reader where the information comes from. In the debating team pie chart example earlier, the source would merely be something like "based on a recent series of interviews by John Smith."

USA Today *has come out with a new survey—apparently, three out of four people make up 75% of the population.*

> —David Letterman,
> Late-night talk-show host

In addition to considering which tools will best present your information, you also need to take your audience into account when you select the tools for your presentation. Marcus learned that the hard way.

Near the end of his first year with a publishing firm, Marcus, an accountant, was asked to make a presentation on cost cutting to the company. Because it was a reasonably large company, Marcus decided it would be more effective to give several smaller presentations to individual departments than trying to speak to the whole company at one time. His boss agreed.

"The first thing I did was decide on an oral presentation instead of a memo," Marcus said. "A lengthy memo on cost cutting could be pretty deadly. I also figured that if I approached each department one-on-one, I could answer questions and my colleagues would be able to put a face on this financial stuff."

Knowing it would be a feather in his cap to pull this off, Marcus planned meticulously. He gathered the figures he would need. He arranged for the use of overheads for pie charts and bar graphs. He even rehearsed his presentation for his girlfriend.

"The first presentation went real well," Marcus said. "The marketing staff seemed to get the message. I got a few laughs. I could answer all their questions. I thought the whole thing was in the bag."

On the very next day the very same presentation was a disaster.

"I was blown away," Marcus said. "Nothing worked. I couldn't believe it."

The presentation had been given to the editorial department. All of Marcus's fancy bar graphs, figures, and tables went over like a lead balloon with people who dealt in the currency of words, whereas they were easily grasped and appreciated by the marketing people, who were more comfortable with numbers. Marcus understood his purpose and goals. He knew his stuff. He rehearsed. What he didn't do was take the time to consider his audience.

"It's the kind of mistake you only have to make once," Marcus said. "I'm glad I made it early in my career."

7 ONCE IS NEVER ENOUGH

The more you know the more you need to know. Especially when it comes to the Internet or nearly anything else related to computers, things are changing too quickly to keep up.

FACTOID:

There are currently 35 million people on the Internet.

Even though the number—35 milion people—in the factoid was accurate when written, by the time you read this more people will certainly have gotten on the Internet. So just because you know something now does not mean it will be always and forever correct.

Recently there has been talk that Egypt—not Greece—was the real hotbed of intellectual activity in the ancient world. Some astronomers have raised doubts about Pluto's status as a real planet. Just when you were sure there were nine planets, huh?

**WHICH OF THESE PIECES
OF INFORMATION ARE
LIKELY TO CHANGE IN YOUR LIFETIME
AND WHICH ARE NOT?**

1. The sun's distance from the Earth?

2. The number of World Wide Web pages?

3. The number of countries in the world?

4. The number of languages spoken in the world?

5. The best way to treat the common cold?

6. The nature of a college education?

7. The fact that your mother and father give you advice on nearly every aspect of your life?

8. The number of bones in a human body?

9. The current world record for running a mile?

10. The number of U.S. presidents who served office in the 19th century?

Only 1, 8, and 10 are unlikely to change over the next 60 or 70 years. Moreover, what's true in one context isn't always true in another, as Jason found out to his embarrassment.

Jason spent a great deal of time hanging out with a church group. The group went canoeing and camping. Once a year the members traveled to a campsite or hotel in a different region of the United States.

Jason worked his way through high school and college as a construction laborer. He usually worked with bricklayers, who took small to medium-sized jobs. He would stock up the bricklayers with brick, block, and mortar. He dug footers and mixed mortar.

Jason had dug many footers in his years as a laborer. Having lived in the South his whole life, he knew that a footer should be between 12 and 18 inches deep, to prevent frost from getting under it and heaving the brick after it settles. He knew his stuff and felt confident as a laborer.

On a church trip up North, Jason's group went out for lunch on its first day in upstate New York. Because the group was so large, Jason and his friends had a 20-minute wait until they could be seated.

While he waited, Jason noticed a construction crew building a house next door to the restaurant.

"I walked over to the guys, you know, wanting to talk one construction worker to another," Jason said. "Two minutes later I felt like a buffoon."

Jason struck up a conversation with a laborer who happened to be digging a footer for the house's front

porch. He told the northern laborer that he was digging deeper than he had to.

"I told him he was already deep enough," Jason
said. "The guy just looked at me like I was trying to be
a smart guy. Actually, I was being anything but smart.
I should have asked a couple of questions instead of
trying to strut my stuff."

What Jason did not know was that just because
something is true at point A does not mean it is true at
point B. You see in the South, footers can be shallower
because it does not generally get as cold as it does up
North. In the North the frost line is at least 36 inches.

"Even though I never worked in construction again
after I graduated from college," Jason said, "I thought
often of the lesson I learned from that little church
trip north of the Mason-Dixon line."

When men are most sure and arrogant
they are commonly most mistaken,
giving views to passion without that proper
deliberation which alone can secure them
from the grossest absurdities.

— **David Hume,**
Scottish Philosopher
and Historian

(Courtesy: Wisconsin Center for Film & Theater Research)

The late film director Alfred Hitchcock quipped about how television bombards us with information when he said, "Television has done more for psychiatry by spreading information about it, as well as contributing to the need for it."

HOW DO I KEEP UP
WITH INFORMATION
WITHOUT GOING CRAZY?

As you know by now, information overload can be overwhelming. Just think back when you, your siblings, and a couple of your friends all shouted different times, schedules, and needs at your mother at the same time. Chances are she shut down, you shut up, and she asked for the information again. Only this time, she demanded to be allowed to focus on one thing at a time.

The same will be true for you. As we have seen in the personal examples, each of the young people had to establish a clear goal before they could successfully seek and find the information they actually needed. Andy had to learn about the shopping habits of mothers and babies; Brendan had to learn more about the wolves of the Rockies; Deleasa had to suddenly manage a new set of information.

By the time you get out of school and have worked part-time jobs, participated in extracurricular activities, and practiced the information management skills discussed in this book, you should have a foundation on which to build. After that, it will be a matter of keeping up with what's new in your field.

Minds are like parachutes.
They only function when they are open.
                    —**Lord Thomas Dewar,**
                              English Wit

Right now, for instance, companies around the world are doing all they can to improve their productivity and their bottom line through the use of computers. If you were in the workforce right now, that's probably where your focus would be. Whatever the situation, you will always be acquiring, evaluating, maintaining, organizing, and presenting information.

Remember this: You will never know all there is to know. It is impossible. The last person who knew all there was to know lived in the 14th or 15th century, and I have forgotten his name because I do not know all there is to know.

Staying current in your field and keeping your mind open to learning more about the world in which you live will be your best way of not going crazy in the Information Age.

(Joe Duffy)

*Technology is a double-edged sword.
Nobody has the rules down yet. People
don't know what type of message to send
for what. The things we use as enablers—
e-mail, the Internet, faxes, voice mail—are
abused and misunderstood and consume
our lives and time. They make the stress
level extremely high.*

**—A'isha Ajayi, Author of
*Understanding Electronic Communications***

GLOSSARY

Database. A collection of information that is organized in some systematic way.

Empiricism. A 17th-century British theory stating that all knowledge is derived from sensory experience, by observation, and experimentation.

Information presentation. A presentation whose primary goal is to convey information on an area of expertise, on technology, methods, procedures, policies.

Internet. The name for the vast collection of interconnected computer networks around the world.

Mail merge. In a word-processing program, a short cut which enables two or more document files to be combined into one file.

Plagiarism. Using (quoting or paraphrasing) somebody else's words and claiming or pretending they're your own words.

Primary sources. Any firsthand information such as a letter written by a former president or an eyewitness account.

Secondary sources. Reports or analyses of information drawn from other sources.

Spreadsheet. A grid made of rows and columns that enables you to organize numerical data and will do complex calculations for you.

Word-processing program. A computer program which helps people edit and type documents quicker and more precisely.

World Wide Web. The name for the interconnected information residing on the Internet.

BIBLIOGRAPHY

Abitebowl, S. *Foundations of Databases.* Reading, Mass.: Addison-Wesley, 1995.

Amadio, William. *The Crisp Approach to Beginning Excel.* Menlo Park, Calif.: Crisp Publishing, 1993.

Arredondo, Lani. *Business Presentations.* New York: McGraw-Hill, Inc., 1994.

Bingham, W. V. D. and B. V. Moore. *How to Interview.* New York: Harper, 1959.

Bowles, Dorothy A. *Creative Editing for Print Media.* Belmont, Calif.: Wadsworth Publishing Company, 1993.

Doniells, Lorna M. *Business Information Sources.* Berkeley, Calif.: University of California Press, 1985.

Fabbri, Tony. *Practical Database Management.* Boston: Kent Publishing, 1992.

Forester, Tom. *The Information Technology Revolution.* Cambridge, Mass.: MIT Press, 1985.

Gillenson, Mark L. DATABASE: *Step-by-Step.* New York: John Wiley and Sons, 1985.

Kay, David C. *Microsoft Works 3 for Windows for Dummies.* Foster City, Calif.: IDG Books, 1994.

Levine, John R. et al. *The Internet for Dummies.* Foster City, Calif.: IDG Books, 1997.

Martin, James. *Computer Database Organization.* New York: Prentice Hall, 1977.

Olsgaard, John N., ed. *Information Science for Library Professionals.* Chicago: American Library Association, 1989.

Pogue, David. *Macs for Dummies.* Foster City, Calif.: IDG Books, 1994.

Schlessinger, Bernard S. *The Basic Business Library: Core Resources.* Phoenix: Oryx Press, 1994.

Schulman, Elayne. *Spreadsheets for Beginners.* New York: F. Watts Inc., 1987.

Sommer, Barbara and Robert Sommer. *A Practical Guide to Behavioral Research.* Oxford: Oxford University Press, 1991.

Still, Julie. *The Internet Library.* Westport/London: Mecklermedia, 1994.

Whalen, D. Joel. *I See What You Mean: Persuasive Business Communication.* London: SAGE Publications, 1996.

INDEX